THE FLYING SENSE

An Ultimate Guide For Pilot Training

A must read for all students who aspire to become a pilot

Sarthak Sinha

This work is dedicated to my late father Capt. R.R.P. Sinha who always enlightened my path with his never-ending support and instilled a romance for flying in my heart & soul.

Disclaimer

Images used in this eBook have been taken from the public domain of commons.wikimedia.org and do not require any prior permission from their respective owners for commercial use. A due acknowledgement is accorded to commons.wikimedia.org and all the owners who have posted their photographs in public domain for the larger interest of public.

The principles or methods describe within this eBook are the author's personal thoughts. They are not intended to be definitive set of instructions. The information provided within this eBook is for educational purposes only. While we try to keep the information up-to-date and correct, there are no representations or warranties, express or implied, about the completeness, accuracy, reliability, suitability or availability with respect to the information, products, services or related graphics contained in this eBook for any purpose. Reader's discretion is advised for any use of the information provided in this eBook.

Any discrepancy in this eBook that may have been crept in inadvertently may be brought in to the notice of the author for modification. Suggestions / comments for further improvement of this eBook may be sent to the author at email: sarthak366@yahoo.co.in.

© All rights reserved: Sarthak Sinha (author)

No part of this eBook may be reproduced or transmitted in any form or by any means, electronic or mechanical, including photocopying, recording or by any information storage and retrieval system, without written permission from the author.

CONTENTS

    Preface

1. The flying sense
2. Relationship between an airplane and its pilot
3. An airplane and a bird
4. Pre-requisites of flying
5. The principle of flight
6. An Airplane
7. The first air experience
8. Glass cockpits - a revolution in general aviation
9. Licences and ratings
10. Careers in aviation
11. How do airlines select and employ pilots?
12. What should pilots do to obtain a flight crew position in a major airline?
13. Important considerations for aiming at a career as a professional pilot
14. Tips for the school students who dream to become a pilot
15. Choosing a correct flying school for your training
16. Medical requirements for trainee pilots
17. Stunning accomplishments by the man in aviation

PREFACE

Before I tell you something about "Flying", I would like to let you know something about machines. Though, the machines are man-made and can be operated on ours' will, yet it is very much alive and vivacious and can hurt or cause an accident if it is misused or mishandled. So, you should be very careful while working with them because you are going to operate one of the most advanced and sophisticated machines ever built by the mankind- 'The Flying Machine'. You should have a sort of respect towards every kind of machines though. In fact, I would say that a machine is your best friend if you know to revere it; but at the same time it might prove dearer to you if it is ill-treated. So, it might be compatible here if I transform a famous proverb as into:-

"A machine is a good servant but a bad master."

Flying an airplane is one of the most beautiful among all the works on earth. It gives you a sense of living, a sense of accomplishment and a meaning to your life. It enhances your self-esteem and gives you a feeling of wholesomeness. It brings you much closer to nature and you start comprehending your surroundings better than ever. So, it is up to you how you receive it. I would advise you to just love it in a true sense and you would get it.

Since you have chosen to be a pilot, I can understand what might be going on in your mind at the moment. You want to fly. Although, you are free to look at flying with your own perspective but I would advise you don't just fly. The word "Fly" here can be elaborated a little in its meaning if you permit me to do so. Before you fly try to resemble yourself with a bird. Fly free like a bird. Enjoy the principles of the nature that has made flying possible. Experience the world which is high up there far from the crowdy earth below which seems more peaceful and soothing than you ever thought. Soon, you would find yourself immersed in an inexplicable beauty of paradise. And if you go to learn flying with this frame of mind then I can guarantee you that you will be the best in your cadre and will surely grasp the lessons very quickly as you have learned how to make flying run in your blood.

Being a pilot is one of the most prestigious professions as very few people have the potential and aptitude to venture in this career. My sincere congratulations to you and wish you a brighter and rewarding flying career ahead. Let's do it.

Happy flying!
Sarthak Sinha

1. THE FLYING SENSE

In fact, when you would start taking flying lessons your instructor would advise you to develop a sense of flying. Well, this is something that you cannot afford to miss if you truly want to be an aviator. Flying sense is actually a kind of sixth sense- a gut feeling that needs to be developed as one of the fundamental qualities in every pilot aspirant. It enables you to foresee snags in aircraft and bad weather conditions well before it takes place and gives you an ability to sniff up the behavior of your aircraft. It makes you cautioned sometimes even before your instruments make an alarm. I hope that the lines written below shall indeed prove of great worth to you. So keep all your senses wide-open.

WHAT IS FLYING SENSE?

There is a word which has a very important place in every pilot's dictionary- "Feeling". This single word has got a plenty of things to do in your flying career. Well, that you would be able to understand yourself. The message that I want to convey to you is that – **you fly with a feeling.** Never ever forget this phrase; in fact, I love it so much that I would not bother if you mind me repeating it once again for you- "FLY WITH A FEELING."

If you cannot feel your flying you can never be a fine pilot. In fact, you might ask me what does a pilot have which you don't have. Well, I would counter that the pilot has got a sense of flying which he has acquired after a lot of practice and requisite flying experience. When something nasty happens to his aircraft while he is flying he is the only person who can first sense it before you. Of course, if you are one of the passengers sitting in the aircraft. He can feel what is wrong with the aircraft and how to tackle with the snag. Just imagine a bird which has spread its wings and can feel the pressure and the forces acting on every inch of its wing when it flies. It twists its tail and wings in a coordinated fashion in order to turn in either direction or gain or lose height. Likewise, when you embark into the cockpit consider every part of your airplane as the part of your own body like your eyes, ears and limbs. Try to feel the pressure being acted upon the wings and other parts of the aircraft. Remember, a good pilot is one who knows his aircraft well. He can tell you approximately how much pressure is acting on his airplane in different attitudes and while doing abrupt maneuvers. He knows the limitations of his airplane. He knows how his airplane would react in different weather conditions and what would be the best suited condition to allow his airplane deliver its peak performance. He is well-acquainted with the after effects and the consequences if he goes wild with his controls. As I told you earlier always keep an eye on the limitations of your aircraft and never try to experiment with abrupt maneuvering as it can lead to structural failure unless your machine is built to withstand this enormous pressure and you are trained with proper endorsements in your license to do so.

As of now, you have come to know about flying in the previous pages, I would suggest you to gain all the qualities mentioned above by doing just one thing- love your flying from your heart and soul. Forget everything while you fly and concentrate on the attitudes and the information displayed on the instruments of your aircraft. Here, one thing I would like to add that while concentrating on the different aspects and behaviors of your aircraft you should always have to keep an eye on the weather and your surroundings. In fact, this is what a "Weather Sense" is all about. It is an integral part of the flying and a necessity to a pilot's character. When all the qualities and capabilities of a bird are amalgamated together, a true aviator is born with a sublime flying sense.

In addition, a pilot should also possess a sense of responsibility. It is you who is going to be held responsible for many lives. Well, you might wonder what do I mean by saying 'many lives' when your aircraft has a passenger capacity of only two or four including you. Remember, it is not much of a concern whether you fly alone or with handful of passengers, but you are strictly responsible for the lives flying along with you and the lives of the people living beneath you. The people down there who watch you with their half-opened eyes and take you as an extraordinary dare-devil who flies aircraft with utmost care. This is not all, apart from the lives of passengers and the people down there; you are also very much concerned about the safety of your aircraft either. You are manipulating a machine that is highly expensive and precious for the company you are working for or the flying club you are being trained at. So, during the distress one should try to save lives as well as his valuable flying machine. But when you are caught in a situation where it becomes indispensable to save the lives by letting the aircraft absorb most of the impact- during crash landing- then it is wise to let go the aircraft and save the lives at priority. After all, lives are more precious than any machine however expensive.

Remember you are the only one up there to take a decision- a decision which is quick, safe, well-judged, well-contemplated and taken for everybody's sake. You are the captain of your airplane and you owe the complete responsibility to commandeer your plane in a safer and judicious manner.

After giving a brief introduction of flying sense I hope now you may have an idea of how to get the best out of your flying. Your instructor would rather elaborate it in detail, so keep a mark of it.

2. RELATIONSHIP BETWEEN AN AIRPLANE AND ITS PILOT

The relationship between an airplane and its pilot is like the relationship of two persons bonded together for lifetime. This can never be broken or ripped apart in a situation whatsoever. The airplane is the pilot's ultimate niche of his life and that he can never compromise his seat of passion with anything in this world. The joy, the bliss that he gets being in the cockpit is indescribable.

So, you being a prospective pilot treat your aircraft as your life partner and give the adequate respect it deserves. Remember, your airplane is your mentor, your teacher, thus try to learn something from it every time you sit in its cockpit. Even if you are an ATPL (holder of Advanced Transport Pilot License) and have plenty of flying experience yet your airplane has plenty to impart on you as your instructor. My father had told me once "Every time you go up in air, your airplane teaches you something". In almost every sortie, you encounter a new situation that will add to your knowledge, may this be your feeling, experience, weather, navigation or the behavior of your airplane.

Know your aircraft fully. Try to remember the positions of the instruments installed in your airplane so that you get so acclimatized with orientation of your flight-deck that you could manipulate them even with your closed eyes. This habit does save your time and becomes critical and life-saving while you are in distress. Never imprecate or curse your craft when it develops any snag. Try to reach out to the root of the problem with the help of your aircraft engineer.

3. AN AIRPLANE AND A BIRD

The man developed a die-hard yearning to fly in the sky by observing the birds. Birds inspired man to harbor a dream to fly and to figure out how the world would look like from above. You also want to go up in air and experience the joy of flying resembling yourself with a bird. What a fun that would be! Just unfathomable!

Well, the purpose of introducing this chapter to you is to make you feel like a bird when you fly- to get you conversant with the laws related to flying that have been postulated by nature. There can be no better way to understand these laws other than the nature's own self-made living prototypes. If you are a good nature observer then you can easily make out what the birds have to say. Sometimes they would warn you about the peril ahead and sometimes they would play with you alluring you to go up and fly with them. You can develop an inseparable relationship with the birds that will never fade out should you monitor them carefully. However, the examples explaining laws and the theories pertaining to flight have been dealt in the subsequent chapter; I would suggest you to come up with some of your own examples derived from nature that would support your inference and conclusions of your observation. Remember- A BIRD NEVER CRASHES!

HOW DOES A BIRD FLY?

If you carefully have a look at a bird you would find that its body is streamlined and aerodynamically designed by nature that offers little resistance in air when it flies. The feathers also contribute in minimizing resistance as they are light and supple. Well, you need not to go too deep in their biology; you simply need to understand the conditions that make them fly. A bird flutters its wings and displaces the air to the downward direction, just like a swimmer who displaces water by his arms to stay afloat. This downward displacement or pushing down the air forcefully creates a pressure difference between the upper and lower surfaces of its wings. The pressure above the wing gets decreased or lowered down due to the streamlining and the flapping of its wing. At the same time pressure under its wing increases and the wings get sucked up into the air. The forward motion of a bird is gained because it is able to flip its wing with a little twisting action in the forward direction with its front edge.

Lift

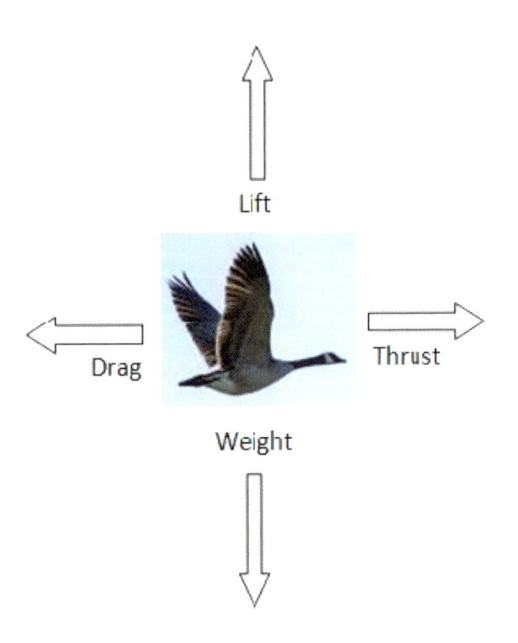

Drag

Thrust

Weight

Birds also encompass some of the natural controlling surfaces that help them make a turn, climb, descend and do awesome maneuvers that will drop your jaws down. These natural controlling surfaces are their tail, flexible tendency of their wings with fanning ability as it stretches out like our five fingers stretched outward.

If a bird has to turn left it just twists its left wing tip upward and the right wing tip downward and make a turn accompanied with a coordinated twisting action of its tail in the left direction. This tail twisting acts as a rudder in airplane which does not allow the bird to fall on its nose and help carry out a well-maintained turn. If it has to turn right it does just the reverse of the above process and vice versa for the left again. The predators like Vultures, Kites, and Owls etc. are also capable to carry out difficult aerobatic maneuvers when they are after their prey. These confounding maneuvers are just impossible for a man to imitate. In fact, it looks quite complicated for us to understand the principles of flying; a bird never gets appalled of this complication and gets accustomed to fly fearlessly. And it must be because that is what it is made for.

They also have a very strong sense of navigation. You will be astonished to know that Siberian birds that migrate to India follow the Rhumb Line track to complete their itinerary. This Rhumb line track is the shortest route to travel and is frequently used by the pilots. But how come these birds know this line? Who taught to them about this line? How are they able to carry out their navigation so flawlessly? Well, the answers might be interesting and mind-boggling but would indeed be one of the mysteries of the nature. Many facts might still be hidden about these birds. They are capable to forecast the weather and can react accordingly. This reaction might help aviators to predict weather in the lack of appropriate instruments or just for having an ability to make approximate weather forecast. They do not know the classification of the clouds or the conditions necessary for forming a fog or thunderstorms; but yet they can sense and anticipate the change in weather conditions by their God-gifted ability to feel.

At the end, I would say that the bird is a master piece of flying that will remain unchallenged and undeterred forever. You can never be a bird but you can indeed try to feel like a bird and emulate them.

4. PRE-REQUISITES OF FLYING

Although, there have been a number of prerequisites or requirements to become a pilot but the most important attribute is your die-hard determination and dedication towards flying. Some of the attributes have already been discussed in the previous chapters. But the rest of them are explained one by one for you. Just keep a note of them.

1. Sharp mind: You should be smart enough to grasp the lessons taught by your flying instructor. Principles of forces, Fluid mechanics, Bernoulli's theorem, thermodynamics, mathematical and analytical skills, they all come handy while learning the principles of flying and understanding working of its state-of-the-art engines. Every word spoken out by your instructor while conducting your training is worth remembering in order to develop a firm hand on the control stick of your airplane. For example, if your instructor says, "When the control wheel or control column stick is turned left the left aileron goes up and the right aileron goes down", just keep this in mind and make a note of every lesson you receive after completing the sortie for ready reference. This will help you to recall the lessons more quickly and will enable you to befriend your aircraft more easily. Regular practice of mental maths such as solving problems of

addition, subtraction, multiplication and simple numericals without the help of a calculator shall sharpen your mathematical skills.

2. Quick reflex action: A sudden natural human reaction or spontaneous corrective activity to avoid any casualty, danger or bodily injury is known as reflex action. Consistent thinking and correct practice shall improve reflex action executing capabilities. You may have to change your course suddenly or ascend or descend in a fraction of a second in order to avoid collision with any other aircraft heading your way and might crash into you or any obstruction lying ahead such as hill top, a bird, Cumulonimbus cloud (Thunderstorm cloud) or a man-made hindrance like an electric cable or tower or bridge or even tree. Extra caution should be exercised while flying low. A quick reflex action saves lives.

3. An aptitude to take decisions: You must possess an aptitude to take a correct decision in limited time. It should always be kept in mind that a decision taken by you as a pilot-in-command in order to save lives would be adjudged rightly and would be taken in good spirit even though it might infringe any law or regulation. I am sure, this aptitude can bring you back on earth safely and can enhance the faith and trust of your piloting among the passengers and your seniors. Raise your self-confidence up to a level where you could turn the situation to your side. **But never be an**

over-confident. You can check this by doing a regular practice of handling tricky situations.

4. An ability to handle more than one data at a time: A pilot flying in difficult weather conditions may have to take note of plenty of information displayed on his flight deck i.e. his airspeed, altitude, direction in which he is heading (course), temperature of the piston heads of his engines, oil pressure, oil temperature, carburetor cooling, airplane attitude, and et al at regular intervals of time. Simultaneously he also has to transmit his position, altitude, course of heading and other relevant information on radio to the Ground Control Station. He also has to ask about traffic clearance, information regarding weather conditions, air pressure etc. in order to plan his flight, all in quick succession. So, you should have good skills to remember the information and have an ability to transmit and receive the numerical data correctly.

5. Positive attitude: Never let negative thinking overpower you, even when you are caught up in an arduous and difficult situation. There is always a way out of that situation should you try to ponder on it keeping your cool. Always look for the positive side. You are the pilot and you have practiced flying to your best to resemble a bird. And bird never crashes. Soon you would find out a solution and can extricate your airplane off the ugly situation. It all depends upon how long and how far you can think optimistically. So

stick in there with your attempts. It does pay and is worthwhile.

6. A cardinal endowment for flying: There should be a never ending love with flying. Because if you cannot love the flying you cannot love the aircraft and hence you cannot be a good aviator. So your aircraft should be your next immediate spouse.

7. Advantage of being vigil: Sometimes even an air traffic controller can deliver you wrong data. So always remain careful and use your flying sense to evaluate the data received from the air traffic controller with the actual weather conditions you are facing and or with the behavior of your aircraft. Never put a blind faith on any information unless you have rechecked it and verified it for yourself. Sometimes even your flying instruments can furnish wrong data so while you fly develop a habit of keeping a cross check on all the information being delivered to you and also those that you had collected before your flight on ground.

8. Good communication skills: Now you already know that a pilot has to establish contacts with Air Traffic Control or ground station or with an aircraft to make sure his appropriate and correct compliance of his flight plan and safety. You must have better communication skills. Since the conversation on the radio is done in English throughout the world your English should be of a class. There should not be

a pinch of stammer or stutter in your voice as it might create confusions among the speakers and may also make an undue delay in communication. Choose words and phrases wisely as stipulated in the flight radio operator's regulations. Practice to speak out English sentences in a decisive, clear tone and has a comprehendible speed without any aberrations.

9. Making Pre-flight checks: Before you get into the cockpit make an express habit of making a complete check of your airplane. Check the lifting surfaces, empennage (tail section), undercarriage and other structural checks recommended in the aircraft manual of the particular airplane. Likewise go for all the checks after being in the cockpit like flight instruments checks, altimeter settings, radio checks etc. I would specifically recommend these checks to be carried out even when one of your trainee friends might have just landed and the engine is still idling and you are about to make a sortie. Never should you try to compromise on these checks. Convert your eyes into an expedient aircraft scanner and give as much time in 'check drills' as it requires.

10. Observing the nature: Be a staunch lover of nature. Try to comprehend what the clouds, the birds, the air have to say to you. Listen to them. Use your flying sense and determine the weather conditions you might face after air-

borne. A good pilot has this ability that sometimes proves to be life-saving whether on ground or in air. So, watch out for the nature.

5. THE PRINCIPLE OF FLIGHT

Any pilot cannot fly his airplane correctly and safely without having a profound knowledge about how does his airplane fly. It is an imperative part of an every pilot's qualification to know about the principle on which he is flying. He should have a clear understanding about the flying techniques, performances and limitations that vary from airplane to airplane. If you comprehend the basic principle of flying, you would exactly be able to say how a big airplane would behave in air as compared to a smaller one in the similar weather conditions. You can easily speculate about the performances of different airplanes even should you have not flown those planes ever in your life.

Today, the technology is revolutionizing the world of aviation and breaking all barriers come in its way. You may even fly an airplane having rudder designed at the bottom of the fuselage, but the principle of flying would always remain the same. Every future airplane, however advanced, will have to follow the same principle. So go through this chapter keenly. It might prove to be your life-long proposition.

Forces responsible for an airplane to fly:-

There are four forces that actually help an airplane sustain its flight:-

1. Lift.
2. Weight.
3. Thrust.
4. Drag.

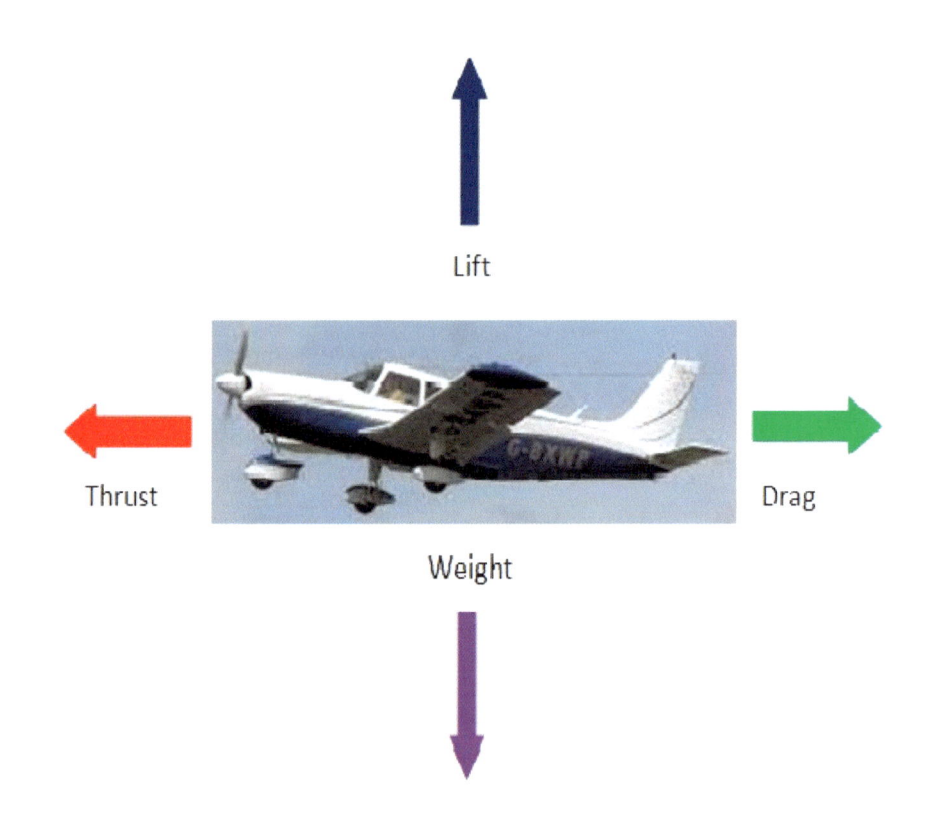

Lift

Thrust

Drag

Weight

1. Lift: - The force acting upward that holds an airplane in air is known as "Lift".
2. Weight: - As the word itself entails, the force acting downwards due to the gravitational pull of Earth is known as "Weight".
3. Thrust: - This force acts in the forward direction caused by revolving propellers or jet engines that make airplane maintain its forward motion.
4. Drag: - This is a resistant force that acts in the backward direction and tends to slow down the forward motion of an airplane. It is opposite to the thrust.

WHAT KEEPS AN AIRPLANE IN AIR?

In the olden days, before the advent of an airplane it was a common belief that anything which is heavier than air could not sustain in air. This notion grew stronger after Sir Isaac Newton; the famous physicist who gave his popular three gravitational laws. So, people were looking for some anti-gravitational force that could act exactly opposite to gravity and could throw things up in air. But the legendary brothers- Orville Wright and Wilber Wright popularly known as "Wright Brothers" broke this jinx what was once looked impossible. Fighting with the same gravitational problem they succeeded in flying a prototype blimp "the Wright Flyer" at Kitty Hawk, North Carolina, USA just by pushing the air back and gaining lift; a principle somewhat analogous to a swimmer who pushes water to his back with his palm and legs and gain a forward motion that keeps him afloat.

The first flight of mankind

This principle can be easily understood by the following example:

Take a square piece of paper. Hold this paper at its ends by both of your hands, take it closer to your lips and blow air forcefully over the sheet from your mouth. What would happen? Well, the sheet will rise up in the air and will flutter until you stop blowing or reduce the speed of air blown. This was a simple experiment illustrated for you to have a clear concept of theory of flight.

The same thing happens with the aircraft. When the wings are allowed to move through the air horizontally the air passing over the wings gets adhered to the upper surface of the wing owing to its bulge for some distance and in the process the speed of the air gets increased. As a result, there is a considerable amount of decrease in pressure over the upper surface of the wing and the wing eventually gets sucked up. You can understand this phenomenon very easily should you have a concept of Bernoulli's Theorem or the principle associated to the Venturi Tube.

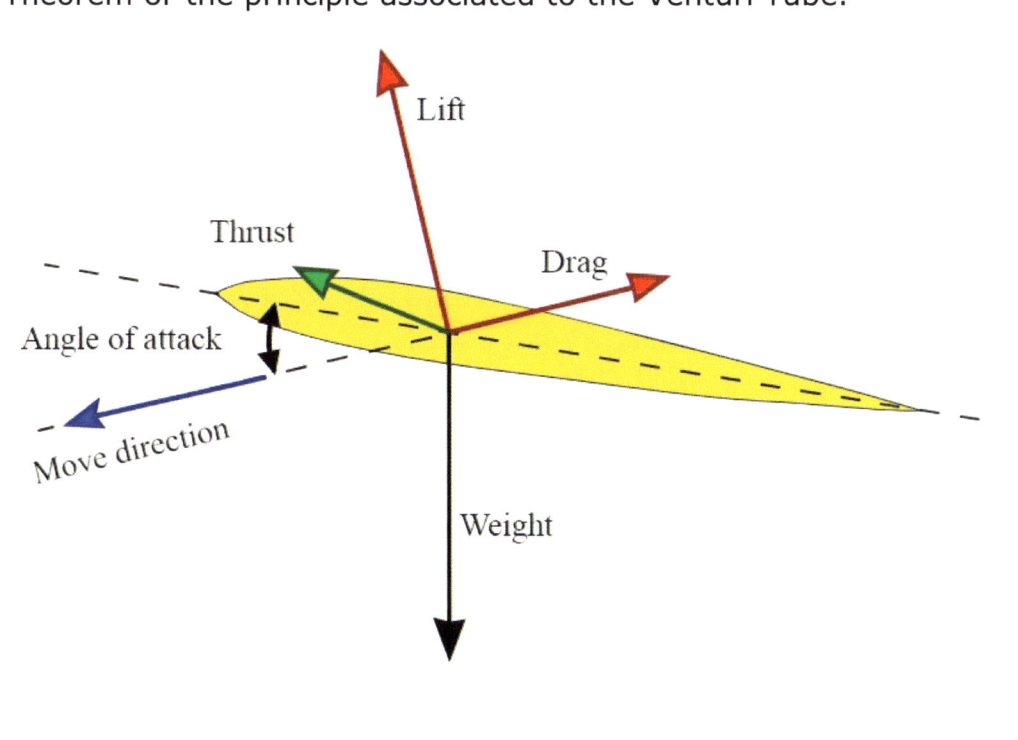

It has been found that this reaction is generated conveniently if the wing has a curvature on its upper and lower surfaces. This curvature is known as the *'camber'* of the wing. The upper camber is often greater than the lower camber of the wing.

AXES OF AN AIRPLANE:

Every airplane is maneuvered around its three axes. These three axes are imaginary lines that are intrinsically associated with any kind of movement of an airplane in air. They pass through the centre of gravity of your airplane.

1. Horizontal Axis: This axis is an imaginary line that passes through the entire length of the wing span from left wing tip to the right wing tip. Ascent or descent of an airplane controlled by elevator is supported by this axis. This up and down movement of the nose of your airplane around horizontal axis is known as "Pitching".

2. Longitudinal Axis: This imaginary axis joins the nose or better the tip of the spinner of the propeller to the end of the tail and passes along the length of the fuselage. The left bank or the right bank controlled by the left and right ailerons is supported by this axis. This movement of left bank (turn) or right bank around the longitudinal axis is known as "Rolling".

3. Vertical Axis: This axis penetrates the fuselage of your airplane and stands erect passing from the bottom to the top of it vertically. The deflection of your airplane to left or right direction controlled by the rudder is supported by this axis. This motion of deflection while changing directions around / vertical axis is known as "Yawing".

AIRPLANE'S CATEGORIES:

Airplanes are categorized generally in three categories:

1. Normal category.
2. Utility category.
3. Aerobatic category.

1. Normal category: An airplane falling in this category is restricted to carry out any harsh movement or rough maneuvers in air. Normal category airplanes are designed to take-off gently, cruise level and straight and land like an amiable cow.

2. Utility category: Airplanes of this category are permitted to go for few specified hard maneuvers in air. These include free stalls, spins, steep turns, lazy-eights etc. All these maneuvers must be performed at the aircraft's minimal reduced weight or when the

airplane is least loaded and should be executed above 5000 feet of altitude.

3. Aerobatic category: The airplanes falling in this category are designed to withstand the heavy loads on its structure being imposed by the gravity especially during abnormal flights. They are built to tolerate as much as 20g's. The pilot would die at this very 'g' stage but the airplane would yet be flying without any signs of hazard. You can unhesitatingly move the controls as abruptly as you can. There would not be any structural failure or fatigue. You should, however, remember that a human being can tolerate only up to 9 g's and that too with a pressure suit. Beyond this mark it would be a suicidal affair. Some aerobats after rigorous practice get so accustomed of such gravitational load that they make themselves tolerant of apparently coping up with the maneuvers that produce 9 g's effect without any preventive suit or aid. You can often find these pilots taking part in World Aerobatic Championships, Air rallies or in different air shows.

6. AN AIRPLANE

Today, each airplane is a master piece and a designer's marvel. Airplane designers leave no stone unturned in order to make their prototypes safer and airworthy. The trainee pilots may not experience any trouble and snag with their airplanes while training. But that does not mean the pilot should rely fully on the aircraft merely because it is newly purchased or having a valid certificate of airworthiness or the reasons whatsoever. You should always keep one thing in your mind that you are flying a machine which needs to be flown with great care and under proper vigilance. Thus in order to fly the aircraft safely and enjoyably it is vital to have a fundamental knowledge of its components, functions, structural design and limitations of its tolerance in different conditions of flight.

By definition, "an airplane is a power-driven flying machine which derives its lift from an aerodynamic reaction on its lifting surfaces." Here lifting surfaces attribute to the different parts of the airplane especially the wings, stabilizers, empennage etc. that help the airplane hang in the air.

Structural parts of an airplane:-

Basically an airplane has the following mandatory components:-

1. Fuselage (the middle body).
2. Wings (the lifting surfaces).
3. The Engine (the propulsion system).
4. Empennage (the tail section).
5. Landing gear (the undercarriage).

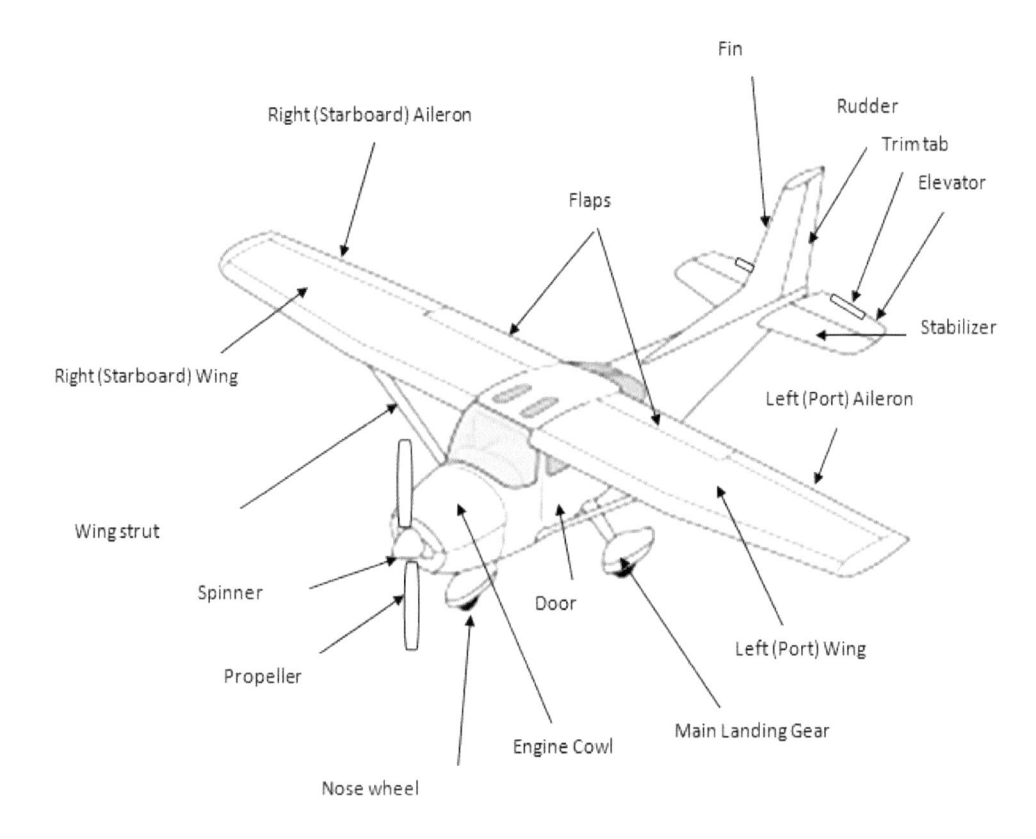

Parts of an airplane

The Fuselage:

The fuselage or the main middle body of the airplane is the most important structure building component. Wings, wing bracing strut, landing gears etc are attached and supported by the fuselage. It is designed to accommodate the specific number of passengers, crew or the cargo up to a certain weight.

The fuselage is classified into different categories depending on how they are designed, material used etc. The two famous categories are the "Monocoque" and the Truss Type".

Wings:

Wings are only meant to generate lift for the airplane and make it turn. They are sometimes even designed to carry fuel, the undercarriage (retractable undercarriage generally) or the arsenals for war purposes especially in the military airplanes. They are made streamlined to reduce drag (friction) and aerodynamically competent in order to produce as much lift as possible.

The principle: When a wing is subjected to forward motion into the air, the air pressure above the wing starts decreasing. It is due to the aero-dynamic design of the aerofoil. Actually the air hitting the leading surface of the wing gets deflected upward due to its slight convex shaped design emerging at the leading edge or the "Camber", thus resulting in the decrease in air pressure on the upper surface of the wing. In contrast, the air pressure at the bottom of the wing is not that low due to the lesser camber of the wing. So the air does not get deflected or pushed downward, thus causing an increase in air pressure to the bottom of the wing. This theory can also be very simply explained by 'Bernoulli's Theorem" in physics. This pressure difference between the upper and lower surfaces of the wing makes an airplane go up. The high pressure below the wing pushes the wing upward as the pressure above the wing is much smaller than the pressure underneath. This is how an airplane lifts off in air.

Airplanes may have high wings, mid wings or low wings and thus the airplanes are also classified as *high wing plane, mid wing plane and low wing plane.*

A typical high-wing airplane

When the wing is attached to the upper surface or the top of the fuselage then it is known as the high wing airplane.

A typical mid-wing airplane

When wings are fitted at the mid of the fuselage, it is known as the mid-wing and similarly when the wings are braced at the bottom of the fuselage it is said to be a low-wing airplane. Low-wing airplanes are generally reinforced to facilitate pilots and passengers to walk over it in order to embark into the cockpit. The wings are normally marked as "step in here" or the like for stepping over it.

A typical low-wing airplane

Now, it is apparent that the classification of the wing is based according to its camber, wing-tip design, material used in its construction etc. There is another kind of wing- which I like the most- the laminar aerofoil. This is actually a high-performance wing especially meant for the aircrafts of higher speed and lower drags. These laminar-flow airfoils are low drag producing as the cambers of both the upper and lower surfaces of its wings are approximately equal resulting in an increased speed.

THE ENGINES:

The engine is a power house of an airplane. It constitutes the propulsion system that actually propels an airplane go forward into the air and help wings generate adequate lift. It generates "Thrust", which is an integral part of the four forces and is one of them acting on an airplane while it is in the sky. The details of these forces and there consequences are explained in the chapter "The Principle of Flying."

An engine may be a piston engine, turbine engine or a jet engine. It may have propellers or without them as in a jet engine. Airplanes may also be classified as single-engine aircraft as if it has one engine or multi-engine aircraft if it is fitted with two or more engines.

Engines are classified according to the number of cylinders installed, their directions of placement or installation, fuel used etc. They can also be sometimes named as Internal Combustion Engine or External Combustion Engine. The piston engines having propellers in the airplanes are all internal combustion engines where ignition of the charge or the mixture of the fuel and air in required ratio takes place inside the cylinder. In external combustion engine ignition of the charge occurs at some other place like furnace and not within the cylinder; the example is Locomotives.

You are requested to go through this subject seriously during your training and make yourself familiarized with the conditions and factors responsible for its smooth running.

THE EMPENNAGE:

The empennage is the tail unit or tail section of an airplane. This back section of the fuselage is encompassed with the supporting and control surfaces like Stabilizers, Elevators, Elevator tabs, Fins, Rudders and Rudder tabs.

The use and functions of these components are explained below:

STABILIZER:

This component keeps the tail of the airplane flying. It is designed similar to a wing that generates enough lift to make it talk with the main wings that makes the airplane fly steady and straight. It may also be made movable in some aircrafts in order to vary the amount of lift produced and thus allows the aircraft to ascend or descend. They function like elevators in such cases.

ELEVATOR:

Elevators act as a resistance to the uniform flow of air over the stabilizer and flip the airplane up and down depending on the upward or downward force applied on its surface after they are deployed. They control longitudinal stability of the airplane.

TAB:

Larger airplanes have larger elevators, rudders and thus the larger control surface area. The control surfaces of an airplane during flight experience enormous pressure making it difficult for a pilot to manipulate them in the desired direction. Thus, they are provided with a small tab that actually moves in the opposite direction of the control surface. This tab may be directly connected to the control yoke. When the pilot pulls the yoke the tab connected to the elevator is deployed downward and resists the airflow under the elevator creating a negative pressure difference and hence making the elevator go up. The airplane starts climbing in the air. This way a tab enables a pilot to steer the aircraft in desired direction by applying relatively much smaller force to the control wheel and preserves the pilot's precious energy. The same principle implies when this tab is incorporated with the ailerons or the fins; only their function gets changed. Control surfaces are also controlled by hydraulic system in the larger aircrafts for smooth manipulation of controls by pilots.

Trim tabs are no different than usual tabs incorporated with the control surfaces. Even smaller airplanes have tabs generally fitted to the elevator for trimming purposes. They are meant to keep the airplane in a specific attitude of flight. They are used during take-off, while leveling out the airplane in air, keeping airplanes in specific flying attitude like maintaining steady climb, leveled cruise or while landing. These trim tabs are controlled by a trimmer fitted in the instrument panel in the form of a stick, wheel or levers. The trim tab is set in a desired angle (nose-up or nose-down) with the help of its trimmer fitted inside the cockpit in order to reduce the pressure on the control column stick and makes the airplane remain fixed in that specific attitude (nose-up or nose-down) depending whether the airplane is taking-off or preparing to land. It may also be used when you have climbed to your desired altitude and now you need to level out your airplane. Adjust the trimmer to the required extent and you would no longer require to keep pushing or pulling your control stick (except in gusty or violent wind conditions) to make your airplane go smooth and level without any signs of ascent or descent.

FIN:

Fin is fixed, long, vertically erected component situated at the top of empennage. It controls the directional stability of the airplane. It is slightly off-set to the right to compensate the left-turning tendency of the airplane caused due to the torque produced by the spinning propeller in the clockwise direction, if seen from inside the cockpit.

RUDDER:

This part of the airplane helps you change directions in which you are heading. It is fixed with the fin and controlled with two rudder pedals inside the cockpit, operated by both legs. When the left rudder pedal is pressed the rudder surface attached to the fin deflects to the left and creates an air pressure that eventually turns your airplane to the left direction. Likewise, the same principle is applied when the right rudder is pressed that makes the rudder deflect to the right eventually making your airplane yaw to the right direction. It is often used with the co-ordination of the ailerons while making turns to either direction to prevent the nose drop of your airplane in the direction of turn.

UNDERCARRIAGE:

The undercarriage or "Landing Gears" are the wheels of your airplane. They provide mobility to your airplane when it has to to be maneuvered on the ground or when it has to make a landing, take-off or taxing out.

There are two types of landing gears:-

a) Fixed or Non-retractable undercarriage.
b) Retractable undercarriage.

Fixed undercarriage:

These landing gears are often found in small airplanes and the trainee pilot would first like try hands on such airplanes. They remain fixed in one position and do not fold back even after the airplane takes off. Thus they offer unnecessary air resistance or parasite drag to your airplane and also affect its over-all speed quite significantly. But all these stuffs are the engineers and designer's headache; you need not to bother about. It would not harm your airplane or its performance because it has been built accordingly taking all these negative aspects and factors into consideration.

Retractable undercarriage:

These undercarriages or landing gears are mostly found in larger airplanes. However, small airplanes do also have such landing gears in order to fulfill the demand of greater speed and better air-performance. It is all up to the designer who designs and gives shape according to the requirements the airplane is supposed to possess. Retractable undercarriage can be found in the large airliners such as Boeing 767, 777, 747, 737, Airbus A-320 etc. or in combat aircrafts like F-16, F-22, MIG-29, etc. Some helicopters also have the retractable undercarriage to achieve their purpose. They are so designed that after taking off you can retract the undercarriage back into the closet built in the bottom of your fuselage or under the wings (depends upon its design) just by pressing a control button or switch or pulling a lever provided in your control-panel. While landing, after getting into the final leg all you need to pull a lever to its erected position and the landing gears would start coming out to take the full weight and jerk of landing as your plane touches the ground.

7. THE FIRST AIR EXPERIENCE

When a candidate gets enrolled in a flying school he is often given his very first flying experience what is known as "THE AIR EXPERIENCE". The flying instructor takes the candidate in air with himself to make him familiar about the aircraft and the feeling of being in air. Following is given the conversation between an Instructor and a candidate named "Rajiv". The training aircraft used here is the "Cessna 172P Skyhawk." Few of the details might vary if compared with the other variants of this plane. However, this plane has an upper hand if compared to its peers like Piper Cherokee, Beechcraft Musketeer or Diamond DA40. The Skyhawk is said to be extremely stable during flight with the latest flying instruments that adorn its flight deck. Some of the upgraded versions of these planes like Cessna 172S have updated avionics package with Garmin G1000 Glass Cockpit. The Cessna 172P Skyhawk, would, however, make it conducive for you to understand the basic principles involved in flying and would offer you a broader perspective on what it takes to be a pilot.

Instructor: I welcome you as a trainee pilot in this flying club. I am quite sure that if you go through the entire training watchfully, you will be able to understand the core things that would come across during the course of your training. I wish you all the success in your training. But make sure that you got to be regular in all of its aspects.

Rajiv: "Sir, I shall indeed try to come up with my best during my training."

Instructor: "Rajiv, We have six trainee airplanes in this flying club- four are single engine Cessna 172 Skyhawks which are tricycle planes, one is twin engine Diamond DA 40 and one is a turboprop KingAir 90 which is a twin-engine aircraft and needs sophisticated hands on its controls. You would be training on Cessna 172 Skyhawk initially and as you would be gaining sufficient air experience you would try your hands on Diamond DA 40 and of course the KingAir."

Rajiv: "Sir, I am excited to start my training!"

Instructor: "Rajiv, I end today's introductory session of yours with a warm welcome once again to you to this flying club. Report tomorrow morning at 7 sharp for your "First Air Experience".

Rajiv: "Roger Sir!"

Next morning the flying instructor turned up on time and found Rajiv waiting for him anxiously and curiously for getting air-borne for the first time.

Instructor: "So, Rajiv, are you ready to get the much coveted first air experience this morning."

Rajiv: "Oh! Yes sir, I have been waiting anxiously for that moment."

Instructor: "Alright, Rajiv, I will take you first to your flying machine in the hangar so that you can get a closer look of your machine before embarking upon it.

"See, this is your machine, Rajiv. This machine is known as 'Cessna 172P Skyhawk'. She has been manufactured by Cessna Aircraft Company with its headquarters in USA. She is of high strut braced wing. The whole body of this machine has been covered with fabrics. She has got three wheels to move on to the ground which is also known as 'Under-carriage' or 'Landing gears'. Two main wheels having tyre pressure from 13 to 15 pounds per square inch and a nose wheel of solid rubber type steerable through the rudder balance cable. If you operate the rudder pedals in the cockpit you can turn the machine in your intended direction over the ground.

Flight Deck of Cessna 172 with analog instruments

Garmin 1000 Glass cockpit of Cessna 172

Now Rajiv, I will take you into the cockpit.

See, this is known as 'control yoke'. It is also known as 'control column'. It is used to control the machine through her correct angle of bank and elevation. While flying, you can operate it in four different ways. If you press the control column forward, the aircraft shall be in a nose down attitude. Similarly, if you pull it backward, you will find the aircraft climbing up. Now, if you press the control column towards left or right, you can bank the aircraft towards the left or right.

These two pedals are the 'Rudder Pedals'. If you press it through your left leg, it will put the aircraft into "Yawing" motion towards the left. Similarly, if you press the right leg pedal, the aircraft will 'yaw' towards the right. Now you can see the upper part of the rudder pedals, it is operated by the tow of your shoes. They are the brake pedals operated by tows that control the main wheels by providing a braking action on both the main wheels simultaneously or together. It also helps the pilot while maneuvering the machine on the ground or to stop the aircraft after making a landing.

Now, I will tell you about the 'throttle' which is provided here as a knob attached to a rod that moves in and out. This is an engine power control system through which we control the engine's r.p.m. (revolutions per minute). It may be pushed in full to get maximum power of the engines. You might have seen an accelerator pedal or a gas pedal in a motor car which controls the power of the engine. Pressing the pedal inward increases its r.p.m. resulting in the increase of speed of the car. In aircraft we call it 'throttle' which is often operated by our hands and not by our feet as it was in the case of a motor car. In a motor car the accelerator is supposed to remain pressed throughout the drive. But here we can fix up our throttle's position to any engine r.p.m. as required. The second thing is if you press the accelerator downward, the motor car speeds up on the road. But in an aircraft it is not necessary that she would gain speed with an increase in power. If your aircraft has a pitch controlled propeller, which is not the case with this aircraft, and the pitch is in neutral position then no matter whatever is the position of the throttle the aircraft shall not move ahead. The aircraft might not pick up speed if you are flying 'into wind' which means flying in the opposite direction of the wind even if the throttle is increased to its full. This behavior of the aircraft is just in contrast to what it normally does in calm air, i.e. the aircraft catches up speed in calm air with the increase of its throttle. You will learn gradually about it as your training progresses further.

The red switch is to select the magneto for firing the engine. Here 'firing' means the ignition of the charge or fuel-air mixture to let it expand inside the cylinder and push the piston back and forth in order to turn the crank shaft of the engine. You can see that there are three positions given- 'L', 'R', and 'Both'. 'L' indicates the engagement of left magneto only. 'R' denotes right magneto and 'Both' uses both the magnetos together.

Rajiv: "Sir, why have these two magnetos been provided while we find that almost all the motor car engines are operated on single magneto?

Instructor: "Good question, Rajiv! The thing is that the entire aviation fraternity vouches for safety. Therefore, two complete ignition systems having dual spark plugs in the cylinders have been provided. In an Internal Combustion Engine, the firing system is termed as the life system of the engine that keeps it running. Both systems work simultaneously with separate sets of control. In case, one magneto fails the other magneto keeps firing the engine and maintains the engine's r.p.m. with a slight drop in it to provide sufficient thrust in order to sustain flight. Another advantage of having a dual ignition system is that it ensures proper burning of the air-fuel mixture in the cylinder and enhances the over-all performance of the engine.

Other components in the fuel system are the 'mixture control knob', 'Fuel cock' and 'Primer'. The mixture control knob controls the amount of fuel entering into the carburetor to provide the best suited fuel-air mixture to the cylinder. When you climb up, the density of the air gets decreased and makes it thinner. This forces us to reduce the amount of fuel entering into the carburetor for optimum performance of engine. The fuel cock checks the fuel supply from the tank. Primer primes the engine by pumping required amount of fuel into the cylinder to facilitate easy and quick engine start up.

Major Cockpit instruments (the 'six packs')

Now, I will tell you about the instruments you see in this cockpit. The first one is a "Timer". The timer displays the time and can be set in accordance with the different time zones viz. G.M.T., I.S.T. The time to which this timer has been set is "I.S.T." or Indian Standard Time. It may also be set as per G.M.T. which is the local time of the "Greenwich" near London. The time being displayed by your wrist watch is approximately five hours thirty minutes ahead the time of Greenwich. You will have the first hand experience about the working of these instruments once you would start flying.

Artificial horizon or Attitude indicator

This half blue and half gray colored instrument is known as 'Attitude Indicator' or 'Artificial Horizon'. It indicates how high or low the aircraft nose is relative to the *horizon.* You must have read about the horizon in your school. Well, the point where the sky meets the earth surface is termed as horizon. If this instrument displays the pointer at the center, it means your aircraft is leveled and straight. It also displays the angle of bank (turn) to the left or right.

Altimeter

This is an Altimeter, which is just an Aneroid Barometer that works on the principle associated with the atmospheric pressure. It is graduated into feet that measure the altitude or the height of the aircraft flying above the ground. Small needle denotes thousands of feet where as the big needle denotes hundreds of feet. Each small division makes for 200 feet. You will have to make a detailed study about this instrument in detail, Rajiv." It is often required to be reset to '0' from the point of take off. The Air Traffic Control provides the local ground level atmospheric pressure over the radio to reset the same.

Air Speed Indicator

Likewise an 'A.S.I.' (Air Speed Indicator) is there to give you your indicated air speed- the speed through which the aircraft is moving in the air. Do notice the colored arcs on the dial that marks the different speed indications.

Slip and Bank Indicator or Turn coordinator

This ball determines if the aircraft is slipping inward, skidding outward or is in the coordinated flight while making a turn to port (left side) or starboard (right side). This instrument that carries the ball is known as 'Turn Coordinator' which is nothing but an inclinometer. The horizontal line appearing over the dial is of 'Turn and bank indicator' or 'Turn and Slip Indicator' which is a gyroscopic instrument in which a gimbal is allowed to rotate freely mounted on a movable axis. The small white arrows signify rate of turn which might be a 1-minute or 2- minute turn to the left or right.

Vertical Speed Indicator

Next is 'V.S.I.' (Vertical Speed Indicator). This instrument is calibrated in feet per minute and registers the vertical rate of climb at which the airplane is ascending or descending.

A typical G1000 Multi Function Display depicting Fuel Flow, Oil Pressure, Oil Temp., Exhaust Gas Temp. & Fuel Quantity indicators

"Next is 'Tachometer'. It shows the revolutions of the crankshaft of the engine or propeller per minute.

Now comes the 'Oil Pressure Gauge'. This instrument indicates the supply pressure of the engine lubricant. It is calibrated in pound per square inch.

The next is your 'Oil Temperature Gauge'. This is graduated in degrees Fahrenheit and gives you the oil temperature readings. This may also be integrated with Oil Pressure Gauge as shown below.

Oil Pressure and Temperature Gauge

This is your 'Cylinder Head Temperature Gauge'. This instrument depicts the temperature of the cylinder head of your engine in degrees Fahrenheit.

The next is the 'Manifold Pressure Gauge'. It is one of the best instruments to measure how much power your engine is producing. The manifold pressure gauge is not about pressure but about negative pressure or suction that a piston of an engine creates while coming back to the bottom of the cylinder, the Bottom Dead Centre. Just ponder over it a little. The cylinders of your engine are big vacuum pump. Every time the piston drops into the "intake" stroke it sucks the air into the cylinder. Your manifold pressure gauge reads this negative pressure or suction created inside the manifold. That's why at idle power your manifold pressure gauge might read 10 or 12 inches of HG when the outside ambient pressure is 30 inches of HG. It is all about creating a vacuum or negative pressure inside the intake manifold.

This instrument reads in inches of mercury or "in hg". The more air /fuel mixture is pumped or pulled into the cylinders, the more power the engine can develop that makes us fly faster. When the engine is shut down, the manifold pressure gauge should read very close to the current atmospheric pressure settings.

And the last but not the least, this is one which is considered to be a backbone for aircrafts especially in navigation and is known as 'Magnetic Compass'. This is a direction indicating instrument and lets you know the direction in which you are heading. This is the most reliable instrument of your airplane. This is nothing but a magnet pointing in the North direction, fixed on a float to which a compass card is attached. This whole assembly is mounted on a pivot within the compass bowl. The bowl is filled with the alcohol to give a buoyancy effect to the float and to reduce the shattering effect during turbulence in flight. Now days, a gyroscopic directional indicator is also provided along with the magnetic compass.

Magnetic Compass

Directional Gyro or Heading Indicator

Today, every aircraft is fitted with a radio through which we can easily communicate with the Control Tower. But in my old days not every aircraft had this liberty. We used to talk to the control tower over a telephone by rotating a lever attached to it from the hangar. Those vintage aircrafts like Tiger Moth, Leopard Moth, Pushpak were not fitted with this remarkable equipment, so we had to speculate all the predicaments of flight we might encounter well in advance while making our flight plan. At those times we often used to fly VFR; i.e. Visual Flight Rules which means that we used to maneuver the aircraft by actually looking through our eyes. Today we can fly without looking outside the airplane by way of IFR; i.e. Instrument Flight Rules.

Now Rajiv, we should be able to know about the weather, which is the most important factor for the flight. See, this is the chart sent to us by the 'Meteorological Department'. According to this report today's weather is normal. In India, flying in the month of September is considered to be an opportunity from the weather point of view. You can also see how calm today's weather is.

Rajiv, you are supposed to make notes of your own of lessons that you learn during every sortie with your instructor. Making one's own note is always considered as a good habit of a good learner.

Always ensure that the aircraft is parked in correct direction. She must be parked 'into wind' that is just against the direction of the wind. Then we should check the airplane from all the corners to ensure she is safe to undertake the flight.

Now we should get into the 'cockpit'. Today I shall be making a circuit flying. A circuit flying encompasses four legs of flying- takeoff leg, crosswind leg, downwind leg, base leg and final leg. I shall be taking over the controls. Your job is only to see, feel and identify objects you observe from the sky, but do not touch the controls.

Now we are going to take off. Take off is always done 'into wind'. Complete the recommended flight checks. You will be told about these checks later in detail. Now, push the throttle full. See that the aircraft is running straight along the center-line. Now, rotate (pulling over the control yoke) – 'Airborne'. Climb up to 400 ft. AGL (Above Ground Level) in the takeoff leg and turn left to crosswind leg and keep climbing to 1000 ft. AGL. Now we are at one thousand feet. Turn left to enter into downwind leg. Notice that the objects are getting smaller and farther. You can recognize objects like the Secretariat building, Golghar- the landmark of Patna and the mighty river Ganges. Those small straight lines are railway tracks. Now I am turning to the left to enter into base leg. From here we would start descending. Now, I am again turning left to enter into the final leg at around 400 ft AGL. And this is 'Runway 25'. We are descending now to touch down.

See that, we have again landed back to the same runway we took off. One should remain vigilant while taxiing out the airplane so that the wing tips of the aircraft do not get brushed up with other planes' wings or any object. So ensure appropriate clearance while taxiing your aircraft. Park the aircraft and switch off the engine. Now, I want to see you tomorrow with a notebook.

RAJIV: "Thank you Sir," he acknowledged with a big smile strewn all over his face.

8. GLASS COCKPIT- FLIGHT DECK MAKEOVER

The technology has gradually forayed in to the cockpits of the trainee airplanes that has conventionally been a thing of the big airliners. The analogue instruments have been integrated in the glass cockpits and are gradually being replaced by these highly advanced digital screens. Today, most of the trainee airplanes have been fitted with these digital screens that provide vital information to pilots. The brand new students begin flying on such aircrafts fitted with technically enhanced cockpits.

A typical glass cockpit

Although, the technology has its own advantages but can also be proved fatal if it malfunctions. Today, the trainee pilots are spending more and more time to get accustomed with this new technology that helps increase 'situational awareness'. Thus they are focussing less on their practical 'flying skills' what pilots used to possess in early days of general aviation. Some advantages and disadvantages of glass cockpits have been enumerated below to enable you to develop an analytical understanding of its pros and cons.

Pros

I mentioned above about the situational awareness that pilots have with the glass cockpits. Some of them are:
GPWS - Ground Proximity Warning System
TCAS - Traffic and Collision Awareness System
Updated Weather - Can receive update weather in some places
GPS - Global Positioning System with moving map
Automation - Automated system.

Cons

The disadvantages that a pilot may face while using the glass cockpit are:

1. The smaller aircraft will have a lessor battery life and shall not be able to sustain the glass screen for long if there is a power failure. This offers a limited time for the pilots to make a decision.

2. Though accidents have been diminished a lot, the likelihood of these accidents is still very much imminent. Since pilots are relying more on the glass cockpit systems rather than their own flying skills, they are more likely to make accidents. This is a major concern all over the flying fraternity as this can be fatal if the glass cockpit system fails.

3. Trainee pilots may find these new systems very cumbersome. They tend to focus on these screens and might be caught unaware of the actual flying and weather conditions being experienced by the aircraft.

4. As discussed above, the glass cockpit system provides an excellent situational awareness to the pilots. But this can only be possible if the pilot is familiar to every function of the system. It is possible for the pilot to get occupied in selecting the correct functions of the system and thus spending lesser time and concentration on flying the aircraft.

5. Switching between the conventional analogue system and the new glass cockpit system can be onerous especially when the pilot has never flown an analogue cockpit aircraft.

6. The glass cockpit alerts the pilot by audible and visual alarms while flying low or in dense air traffic. The TCAS and GPWS raises alarm when the aircraft flies near the ground and comes close to any aircraft flying in its near vicinity. These alarms can become distracting for the instructor and the student during training exercises and could be turned off to avoid the distraction. It may be possible that a student pilot might also learn to ignore these alarms or turn off them and could override these vital signals when there is an actual emergency while flying off solo. This could in turn be critical and might lead to a fatal accident.

In order to remedy the above situations, a pilot must possess the distinguishing capability to correlate the information displayed over the screen and the actual condition the aircraft is facing. Instructors should ensure that their students are not allowed to fly off solo without being fully acclimatized with the glass cockpits and their functions. The young pilots should also be taught to pay proper attention on all the warning signs and alarms of the system and to take corrective action well within time. The pilots should keep honing their flying skills and practice mock drills to stay alert so that taking a correct action during distress could become their regular habit.

9. LICENCES AND RATINGS

You cannot fly any aircraft unless you have the required licences and ratings to fly. To acquire these licences and ratings is what the flying training is all about.

The list of these licences and ratings according to their hierarchy has been drawn as under:-

FIXED-WING POWER DRIVEN AIRPLANE:

Licences:

1. Student Pilot Licence (SPL).
2. Private Pilot Licence (PPL).
3. Commercial Pilot Licence (CPL).
4. Senior Commercial Pilot Licence (SCPL).
5. Airline Transport Pilot Licence (ATPL).

Ratings:

1. Instrument Rating (IR).
2. Assistant Flight Instructor Rating.
3. Flight Instructor Rating.

4. Extension of particular aircraft Rating

ROTOR WING OR HELICOPTERS:

Licences:

1. Private Helicopter Pilots Licence (PHPL).
2. Commercial Helicopter Pilot Licence (CHPL).

Ratings:

1. Aircraft Rating.
2. Night Rating.
3. Extension of aircraft rating.
4. Instructor's Rating.

GLIDERS:

Licences:

1. Glider Pilot Licence (GPL).

Ratings:

1. Aircraft Rating.

2. Aero-tow Rating.

3. Instructors Rating.

10. CAREERS IN AVIATION

After gaining your Commercial Pilot Licence, you can be deemed fit for employment in the General Aviation Industry. There are a number of flying activities you can choose from viz. instructing, freight, aerial tours, charter, mustering, survey joy flights, or flying for the smaller airlines that might translate opportunities for pilots like you to build your flying experience to a requisite level to join a major airline.

COMMERCIAL AIRLINE PILOT:

Every general aviation pilot harbors a dream to fly an airliner in a major airline. This is the most sought-after career and a coveted position in the industry. Now a day, travelling by air has become an indispensable part of every one's life. People have accepted this fastest mode of transport for their business travel, vacations on exotic destinations or simply commuting from one place to other. The demand for highly trained commercial pilots is growing steadily. And because of the stability, working conditions, attractive salary and fringe benefits that exist in this profession, many pilots consider the major airlines their ultimate career destination. Career as a commercial airline pilot might be rigorous and demanding. Flying as a 'Commercial Pilot' can take you across the globe or across the nation and might keep you away from your home for a period of at least six months in aggregate.

Most flight crews are comprised of Captain, First Officer or Co-pilot and Flight engineer or Second officer. Promotion from flight engineer to first officer to captain is usually determined strictly by seniority and flying experience gained over time.

FLYING INSTRUCTOR:

It is privileged to be called as the best career to start with for budding commercial pilots. It is highly rewarding and fulfilling career for the young pilots with little flying hours in their log books. If you have the propensity to teach new budding pilots then this could be your best option to go with. It not only replicates your air experience leaps and bounds but also makes you aware of your negative habits, your shortcomings and weaknesses. A minimum of 1000 flying hours of experience on a multi-engine aircraft is required to switch to any commuter or regional airline. Career as a flying instructor can come handy for the switch over.

AIR FREIGHT OR COMMUTER / REGIONAL AIRLINE PILOT:

Flying as a pilot in an air-freight company or any regional or commuter airline is often considered as one of the stepping stones to fly for a major commercial airline. As outlined above, you may have to work for a flying school or any flying institution as a flying instructor to accumulate a minimum of 1000 hours of flight time that is usually required to be considered for selection as a commuter or regional airline pilot or air freight pilot.

Being a commuter or regional airline pilot, you may get an opportunity to fly larger and more complex aircraft, and this will help build up your overall flying time and experience.

CHARTER PILOT:

The job as a charter pilot may also be considered as one of the modest ways that paves way for a commercial airline pilot. You can join a charter company as Chartered Pilot after having worked as a flight instructor. Working as a Chartered pilot may involve flying different types of aircraft and helps accumulate valuable air experience. Working conditions, emoluments and the types of aircraft flown vary greatly.

CORPORATE PILOT:

In today's competitive market place, many corporations and businesses find it economically viable to own and operate aircrafts of their own. As a Corporate Pilot, you may fly executives across the state or across the country. So, you must have to be ready to roll on a moment's notice. Aircrafts you fly can range anywhere from small single engine airplane like 'Pilatus' to mid- size jets. Some of these companies may operate several aircrafts and can offer a plenty of flying time to pilots. You may choose to work for a large corporation, a large company, a family owned business or even a rich single individual.

You may also start your career as a Corporate Pilot after completing your CPL training. The requisite flying experience earned while flying a multi-engine aircraft for a multi-rating endorsement can be an advantage to secure a job of a Corporate Pilot if the same aircraft is operated by the companies or individuals you intend to work for.

GOVERNMENT OR MILITARY:

After gaining your commercial pilot licence and necessary ratings, you can also opt to become a Government pilot flying aircrafts belonging to the Governmental organizations. Generally, these aircrafts are multi-engine or helicopters because they carry VIPs or VVIPs; so they ought to be safer. In case you vouch to fly important people you must have a required level of experience stipulated in the Aircraft Rules and the regulations.

Preference may be given to candidates possessing valid CPL and other relevant qualifications in the defense entities like Indian Coast Guard, Indian Army (Air wing) and in Indian Air Force.

Pilots relieved from Short Service Commission may also get into the realm of civil flying and continue their career as 'Commercial Pilots' in different organizations.

11. HOW DO AIRLINES SELECT AND EMPLOY PILOTS?

I would like to make it clear that most of the airlines do not sponsor people to learn to fly. So you should plan to undertake your flying training by your own.

Pilot Selection Process:

You may have to go through a rigorous and comprehensive pilot selection procedure. This selection procedure is generally comprised of assessments of your abilities, aptitude, personality, medical fitness and two interviews. The intention behind these tests is only to make sure that the quality of recruits entering these major airlines remains very high. But I do not intend to frighten you up by mentioning about these tests. Absolutely not! In fact, this will defeat the very purpose of this book which is not to appall the students but to arm them with basic knowledge of pilot training so that they could face their training drills however tough and complete them in any part of the world with flying colours.

After being qualified in the above mentioned tests and assessments, you may have to spend between four to six months training with the respective major airline learning flying larger jets and the specific rules and regulations of the airline. Before commencing flying on regular services you will undertake training on the aircraft systems, flying procedures, flight planning, navigation and emergency procedures on the aircraft simulators.

Candidates leave the training school as a Second Officer after having undergone the training successfully.

Second Officer:

Second officers are often carried on long-route flights and they observe Captain and First Officer how to use the inner instincts while flying the aircraft. They notice the important considerations while takeoff, landing and may sometimes fly the aircraft while cruising. This allows the Captain and First Officer to take some rest off the flight deck and adds to the Second Officer's valued flight experience either. So the learning process is always on whenever the pilot enters the cockpit of the aircraft. The knowledge and experience acquired on being a second officer may make him eligible for training for promotion to First Officer. Promotion to First Officer may be offered after holding the Second officer rank and depends on vacancies at the time, seniority, proficiency and the successful completion of promotion course.

First Officer:

First officers are Co-captains or Co-pilots. They make command decisions and judgments while in flight under command and supervision of the captain. First officers are entitled to fly the aircraft during takeoff and landing and in cruise. The promotion of the First Officer to the Captain may be expected within three and ten years after being promoted as the First Officer. The promotion again depends on vacancies, seniority, proficiency and successful completion of the training period that may go up to six months.

Captain

Captain is the supreme commander of the aircraft. He gives directions to the first and second officers to undertake the operations of the flight. He owes an ultimate responsibility for the aircraft safety, the crew, the passengers and the freight.

Vacancies:

Vacancies for pilots are often advertised in the major newspapers, aviation magazines etc. These advertisements include the application criteria and a request for qualified pilots to apply.

Since airlines fall in service industry and thus they also get exposed and affected by the ups and downs both in domestic and international markets. This might result into the growth or the retraction of the vacancies for the pilots. You should be an extra-cautious to grab the opportunity and must not take any job opening casually. Remember, opportunity never strikes your door twice. You must be qualified and ready to apply when there is a suitable vacancy exists for you. Do also remember that a job opening may not be of your type but could be instrumental in paving way to realize your type of job.

Retirement:

Retirement age for pilots flying in different airlines may vary but generally it is 55 years. But you may extend your service to 60 years if you are found medically fit.

12. WHAT SHOULD PILOTS DO TO OBTAIN A FLIGHT CREW POSITION IN A MAJOR AIRLINE

It has always been a difficult road ahead for a new CPL holder to obtain a flight crew position in a major airline. This is because he lacks sufficient flying experience to meet the minimum requirement of the airlines. In fact, this is an important aspect to be considered and one that is often overlooked by student pilots while deciding on training options.

Requirements solicited by most of the domestic airlines may, however, be different for regional and commuter airlines.

Although, it has already been stated in the previous chapter but owing to its importance, I would like to point out once again about the minimum requirement to obtain a flight crew position in a major airline that should always be kept in mind by a student pilots are :-

1. Minimum age 21 years.
2. 10+2 schooling (or equivalent) completed with good grades. It is better if you are a degree holder.
3. Commercial Pilot Licence (CPL).
4. Multi-engine endorsement.

5. Multi-engine Command Instrument Rating.
6. 1000 hours flying experience, including at least 500 hours "in command" experience.

A CPL holder typically has to obtain employment in General Aviation to build up 1000 hours of air experience prior to applying for a job in the airlines. Therefore, your training course must be designed to allow you to expedite your path into employment in the aviation industry and strengthen your career prospects with an airline.

While you finish up your training by obtaining your Commercial Pilot Licence and other relevant certifications and ratings, you are also advised to undertake training for a flying Instructor rating or Assistant Flying Instructor rating. Gaining your first employment in the aviation industry as a Flying Instructor is perhaps the best and the simplest way to begin your aviation career. This rating enhances your flying skills and offers you to obtain high levels of proficiency in all kind of aircraft maneuvers. After undergoing this additional training you may find yourself in a much more employable situation and could be able to pursue your career ahead. This also helps increase your flying experience significantly and opens a plethora of career avenues. After building your valuable air experience and skills you may pursue jobs in air charter and air freight operations.

ADDITIONAL QUALIFICATION:

It would be worth considering completing a degree in other subject areas such as Business Management or Marketing. This actually places you ahead of a typical Licenced candidate willing to apply for a flight crew position and also provides excellent background knowledge to the pilots about the nitty-gritty of how an airline earns profit. The major airlines are now looking closely at qualifications and experience outside the aviation field in their prospective candidates as an advantage to their organizations.

Airlines and other aviation based organizations are all part of the aviation industry. It should be regarded as a full-fledged business organization or centre that requires entrepreneurial brain, business administration, marketing and managerial skills for their smooth and hassle-free operations. If the flight crew have the know-how of these additional subjects then they would surely be able to think not only for themselves but also for the growth of the company and would also be capable of handling customers and enhancing their company's credibility, value-added services and many more in a broad spectrum.

It should, however, be noted that flying schools or institutes in India do not offer much to its students except few like Indira

Gandhi Rashtriya Udaan Academy and some selected schools. They look in professionalism and hardly provide their students the competence, confidence and aptitude to fly and handle air traffic anywhere in the world. Flying schools in India really need an improvement to provide a wide range of experiences for the trainee, including multi-engine high performance aircraft training with the necessary professional education and experience. This will certainly help Indian candidates to be able to fly anywhere in the world and compete with the foreign pilots with high level of precision and accuracy.

It is not bad however to begin your training in India but if you are financially sound and can spend up to around 40 Lacs rupees or more then it would be advisable to gain your flying lessons and experiences abroad like in UK, Australia, USA or Canada. There are some schools in UK and other countries who impart training on the Flight Simulators of Boeing or Airbus range of airplanes often operated by the major airlines for the candidates obtaining training for JAA-ATPL. This gives you preference at the time of your selection in any major airline because of your prior exposure on the aircrafts they operate. It can also help you develop your flying sense and an ability to handle any kind of challenge in the shortest possible time. You also come to know about the fundamentals of the inner workings of the aviation industry and job prospects in different countries according to the Licences and experience acquired.

13. IMPORTANT CONSIDERATIONS FOR AIMING AT A CAREER AS A PROFESSIONAL PILOT

Some considerations have got a significant bearing over your training for a commercial pilot license. This actually decides your career prospects in the long run. It is really very unfortunate that most of the times people make the wrong decisions at the beginning of their training and end up with a lost opportunity for an aviation career.

Following are some fundamental considerations that have to be borne in mind while making your decision:-

If aiming at a career with the major airlines:-

AGE:

The age is the most important factor if you are willing to build your career as an airline captain in a major airline in India or abroad. You should really be an extra-cautious about your age as it might turn all your dreams to soil.

The major airlines generally look to induct young and dynamic flight crew preferably between the age group of 21 and 28. The reason for this is airlines incur huge cost in training these brand new CPL holders to fly jumbo size airliners. So, the lower the age of the flight crew the longer they could serve the airline. This allows the airlines to recover the training costs they have incurred on you.

For this reason, you must not delay or should better avoid any delay in order to secure yourself a position where you could easily be able to apply for a flight crew position.

Training:

You should complete a full course of training that runs no more than twelve months and then commence working for the aviation industry. This will allow you to get yourself acquainted with all the pros and cons of the industry at an early possible age. In addition, a meticulous student can also acquire valuable experience in aeronautical engineering, aircraft maintenance engineering, airport management, marketing etc. that gives him an extra edge. In contrast, should you wish to obtain a degree qualification or equivalent in these subjects then you can also obtain the same while continuing in the job either.

If looking at other career options such as- regional and commuter airlines, flying instructor, charter pilot, freight pilot etc.:-

AGE:

If you have an inclination to work for the regional and commuter airlines or are willing to work as a flying instructor, charter pilot, freight pilot, as you surely have to for building necessary air experience, then you can enjoy few relaxations in terms of your age. You can easily fly for your living at any age subject to your medical fitness. Pilots having attained the age of 60 often find airlines bid them adieu as it becomes difficult for them to maintain the stringent health standards as required by the aviation industry. But if you are medically fit then you can fly at any age.

Training:

Since there is no age restriction, you can fly at any age even if you inevitably encounter any delay in completion of your training. But if you happen to fall between the age group of 21 to 28, you can easily switch over for a flight crew position in any reputed airline after building the requisite hours of air experience.

14. TIPS FOR THE SCHOOL STUDENTS WHO DREAM TO BECOME A PILOT

An aviator's training is believed to be commenced right from the school when a student enters his or her high school. You should have a proclivity towards mathematics and physics especially at standards Eleventh and Twelfth. Please also try to brush up your English. Choose Physics-Chemistry-Maths stream at standard eleventh in order to comprehend the complex but easy to understand principles involved with airplanes and over-all flying. Pass out your final twelfth examinations with good grades having a sound knowledge of how things work on Earth.

Besides the academic part, you should also have an interest in some sort of adventure. Try to go out on any mission or assignment. Enroll yourself in Boys Scouts at your school. This will help build confidence and risk taking ability in you. Do take part in school debates, elocution contests and other school organized events. Watch Discovery Channel, National Geographic, and Science Channel etc. on a regular basis. I used to watch the programs such as Wings, Frontiers of Flight, Extreme Machines, Popular Mechanics for Kids and other educational programs on a regular basis. I am not promoting these programs to increase their TRPs but only advocating learning the basics of flying that these programs have to offer to the budding pilots. Additionally, a lot of stuff is available over the internet where one could easily find videos and reading materials relative to flying.

You should try to develop a quality of leadership to guide others during exigencies and an aptitude to face challenges with a calm and cool mind. You should also try to do some eye-to-hand or eye-to-hand-foot activities like type-writing, car driving; games to build up your muscles such as cricket, hockey, table tennis etc. This will sharpen your reflexes and enhance your flying instinct and aptitude. As I have told you earlier that a pilot's job is full of responsibilities, you should prepare yourself right since the very beginning.

After qualifying your twelfth final examination you can register yourself in any Government or Private Flying training institutes in the country or abroad. But do continue your academic studies and try to get a degree and be a graduate. Many airlines and other aviation organizations prefer graduates. It would be advisable to have a diploma or degree in Business Management or Airlines Management apart from your flying qualifications. This will make you a more employable candidate at the time of your selection in any organization. Try to finish your pilot-training when you reach 21 years of age. This is because after this age you get a plenty of time to build your valuable flying experience by flying any twin-engine aircraft in any small organization operating air Freight or Air-Charter services.

The biggest aim of any prospective pilot who wished to be in 'Civil Flying' is to be a 'Commercial Pilot' in any reputed commercial airline. He gets an opportunity to fly some of the biggest and fastest airplanes in the world of civil aviation. Airlines prefer to absorb fresh, enthusiastic and passionate pilots between age group of 21-27. Thus they get an advantage of having a pilot's full-term service to them and also redeem the value of the expenses incurred on them during their preliminary training for flying the challenging jets in their respective airlines.

School students are advised to undergo full medical examination including a check of your hearing and eye-sight before you choose flying as a career to avoid any future disappointment. A Class One Medical is required to commence your training and is the most important facet on which the entire training depends on. A medical Fitness Certificate is issued from a panel of doctors empanelled by the Director General of Civil Aviation. If a flying career is to be denied to you because of medical reasons, it is best to know before choosing subjects for the final two years of school. Details about medical requirements have been explained in the forthcoming chapters.

PILOT TRAINING- PRUDENCE REQUIRED:

I am pleased to provide you some of the factual information about pilot training that you will find of value and will help you to make the right decision.

Your Goal:

Flying a modern jet aircraft is both physically and mentally demanding. You need to have all the qualities of emergency handling capabilities. You owe a great deal of responsibility for the lives of the passengers on board, the security of the airplane and of course the lives of your crew members and indeed yourself. The details regarding the characteristics and qualities needed to be a pilot are exhaustively elaborated in *chapter-4 'Pre-requisites of flying'*.

Age:

You can actually start your training when you attain 16 years of age. However, the preferable age is between 18 to 27 years.

Nationality:

It is advisable to go through the Indian student selection procedure in case you are opting for a foreign flying school. Some countries have made stringent rules and regulations for inducting foreign student to their flying schools. Some foreign flying schools may interview the prospective students and might also take a written examination to check their mental acumen. However, if your antecedents and clear and have a sponsor to finance your training then you should not experience any problem in obtaining a student visa for the commencement of your training abroad.

Academic ability:

Students who have completed their 10+2 schooling (or equivalent) and have scored good marks in Physics, Chemistry, Mathematics and English are deemed eligible for flying training. It would be an added advantage if you are also good at Geography and have some knowledge about astronomical science. These will help you understand the subjects like Meteorology and Navigation at the time of your training. You should continue your studies till graduation should you wish to become an airline pilot in any reputed airline. You should, however, also be willing to undertake an exhaustive theoretical study and sit for examinations for acquiring requisite licences in different stages.

Physical attributes:
1. Your height should be above Five Feet and Two inches (5'2") with weight in reasonable proportion.

2. You should be physically fit and able to satisfy Indian Medical Establishment of Air Force or IMEAF in India or Civil Aviation Authority United Kingdom or institutions that are responsible for medical fitness of the pilots in their respective countries. Note that the airlines have their own standards of medical requirements before selecting pilots for them.
3. You should also have a normal vision. Wearing glasses does not mean automatic rejection.

Communication skills:

You should have the following:

1. Fluent in English.
2. Clear speaking voice.
3. Confident communicating skills.
4. Ability to win the confidence and co-operate as part of a team.

Aptitude:

1. Close attention to details, particularly when working with figures.
2. Good hand to eye co-ordination and practical aptitude.

3. Analytical and capability and able to understand and apply technical data.
4. Calm under pressure, even when managing a number of tasks simultaneously.
5. Good spatial awareness, with the ability to interpret maps and three dimensional displays.
6. Excellent powers of observation.

15. MEDICAL REQUIREMENTS FOR TRAINEE PILOTS

The pursuit of your commercial pilot license has a direct bearing on your passing the class one aviation medical examination conducted by the Central Medical Establishment of Air Force (CMEAF) at New Delhi. This medical includes a general physical examination, including eye sight and hearing tests. For the reason your entire aviation career depends on passing this crucial examination, you are requested to get your medical exam done in advance to rule out any medical deficiencies for opting to become a pilot.

In Europe or Australia, the authority to determine the medical examinations standards is Civil Aviation Authority (CAA) or JAA. In the United States of America, Federal Aviation Authority (FAA) is responsible for the medical assessments of the pilots.

The following notes are provided as a guide to the CAA class one standards which are only illustrative and not exhaustive. However, many of the reputed airlines do follow these standards as yardstick.

You will be required:

1) To be free from any health condition that may interfere with the safe operation of an aircraft, and from symptoms that may aggravate by working in a changing pressure environment or in different geographic terrains and climatic conditions;
2) To be Free from any established history of psychosis, alcoholism, drug dependence, personality disorder, mental abnormality or neurosis of significant degree;
3) Not pregnant at the time of CAA or any other authority medical examination.
4) To be free from hearing defects;
5) Within the height range of 5'2" to 6'3" (1.57m-1.91m) with weight in reasonable proportion. (Airlines may include their additional requirements);
6) Normal color perception;
7) Normal field of vision;
8) Distant visual acuity of not less than 6/9 in each eye separately, with or without the use of correcting lenses, visual acuity in each eye separately without correction must not be less than 6/24;

All the medical examinations are done by an expert panel of approved doctors and medical professionals authorized by

Director General of Civil Aviation in India or the authority concerned in case of other countries.

16. CHOOSING A CORRECT FLYING SCHOOL FOR YOUR TRAINING

Your flying training school is your first exposure to the world of aviation. It helps you to build a strong foundation over which you intend to pursue your aviation career. The school must help you develop a positive impression about the airplanes which you are going to learn-to-fly. The most important factor that every student must take into consideration is the "Instructor" of the respective flying school. The school should be equipped with a panel of certified instructors to whom students could repose confidence. An instructor must have a willingness to assist students in making them love-to-fly pilots. The school should also make sure its students have access to all of the facilities being offered by it. It should provide requisite assistance needed to its students while training for better results. So, before choosing any flying training school or institute there are many factors that need to be taken into account prior to enrolment. You should, however, meet the instructors, talk to the student pilots undergoing training and enquire about the problems being faced by them, if any. This will give an insight of an overall performance and reputation of the school you intend to select. Before enrolling yourself in any of the flying schools, whether it is Governmental or private, consider about the following aspects:

1. Location:

    It is better to have your flying school in your own city of domicile. This significantly cuts your living expenses, transportation charges and other expenses. In contrast, schools located at far-off places might eventually cost you dearer for your training from all viewpoints. However, if you do not have any flying school at your place then choose the best suitable school feasible to you keeping all the necessary factors in mind.

    Try to choose your flying school located at one of the major cities like New Delhi, Mumbai, Bangalore, Kolkata etc. These cities actually have a major chunk of the air-traffic in India. Selecting schools in these cities help you to be trained in a professional airspace environment right since the very beginning of your training. This, in turn helps you develop skills and experience to be able to fly into the busiest of airports with ease and confidence. Exposure to the traffic on such airports is a valuable part of the training of a commercial pilot. This will make you will feel confident that you can fly in and handle heavy air-traffic airports anywhere in the world.

2. Training program:

Most flying schools offer tailor made courses to their full-time and part-time students. You should, however interview the admissions officer of the school and ask as many questions that you may have like:

(a) What is the vision and objective of the flying school?

(b) Who keeps the flying records of the students?

(c) How is a training schedule prepared and who does it?

(d) What kinds of trainer aircrafts are being used by the school?

(e) How often the aircrafts are maintained?

(f) What are the qualifications of the flight instructors?

(g) Are they DGCA Certified Flight Instructors?

(h) How much time does it take to complete 60 hrs of flying?

(i) Does the school conduct regular classes in its ground school?

(j) Does it have the resources of study materials like books and CDs to enable its students to study at home?

(k) Do they provide insurance to all its students or whether the students have to arrange the same on their own?

It should be borne in mind that all the certifications like Private Pilot License, Commercial Pilot License, Command Instrument Rating, Multi-engine Rating, etc.

must be obtained in the shortest time possible. Although, it depends on your own personal skills and how quickly you grab the lessons in order to complete your training on time.

3. Instructors:

The job of a flying instructor is a different domain altogether. It would be difficult for you, though, to judge your instructor, but interacting with them would open up many realms of your flying aspirations. Talk to your future instructor to know more about the flying school you intend to join. Take a detailed tour of the school and do also interact with the students pilots to know about the innate problems of the school that remain hidden from the outside world. Try to figure out the following qualities in your to-be-instructor:

(a)   They should be superb pilots and good teachers.
(b)   Passion about flying.
(c)   Love to share their specialized knowledge with their students.
(d)   No history of accidents or casualties in the past.

Since flying training is going to be a personal experience between you and your instructor, the institute should associate with you the best suitable instructor who could understand your level of comprehension, flying skills, strengths and weaknesses so that he could remain with you throughout your training to boost you up. In addition, the Chief Flying Instructor should oversee all your training exercises and happily discuss issues with you at any time you need.

4. The fleet:

   The fleet of aircrafts should be diverse comprising of single and multi-engine configurations in order to allow the trainees achieve greater flying experience even on the complex airplanes. In India, the fleet generally includes single engine aircrafts in most of the flying training schools or clubs like Cessna 152, Cessna 172 Skyhawk, Piper etc. There are certain reputed institutions like Indira Gandhi Rashtriya Udan Academy and few others who have the twin-engine aircrafts like Beechcrafts and others.

   You are advised to have as many aircrafts endorsed on your license as possible to make your license "open" in order to make you eligible to fly any airplane that fall within the same all-up weight configuration. CPL trainees must experience a wide range of different aircraft's types during their training ranging from basic trainers to the advanced multi-engine turbocharged aircraft having latest satellite navigation system and other advanced equipments.

5. Recognition and Approval:

    The institute must be approved and recognized by the Director General of Civil Aviation (DGCA) which is an autonomous body under the Ministry of Civil Aviation, Government of India. It conducts examinations of various flying Licences and certifications in India. In case of selecting any foreign school it should be made ascertained about its recognition and validation from the concerned authority from its respective country.

6. Training cost:

    The overall training cost may vary considerably depending upon the flying school, its fleet of aircrafts, their operation, and the facilities provided therein. In India, the non-subsidized training cost might range between Rs. 15 to 20 Lacs calculated at Rs. 10000 per hour approximately. Subsidy offered by the Government might curtail this sum to even one-fourth or 5 lacs or something. Since the training cost is subject to change as it depends on the cost of operation of the aircrafts, cost of ATF and others, you are advised to consider this factor as an integral part of your training. However, the banks like State Bank of India offer education loan for your training as against the collateral bequeathed by you or your parents.

7. Facilities:

The institute/school should combine all pilot training facilities. This may include fully equipped class-rooms, well-equipped video library, Flight simulators, study areas, briefing and dispatch areas, testing, planning room with fax, telephone, and internet facilities. This may also include the latest computerized audio visuals aids for more sophisticated training.

Institute may have meal facilities, boarding-lodging and transportation facilities included in the training fee or give it as an option depending on student's discretion.

8. Foreign Flying Schools:

If you are planning to commence your training in the flying school of foreign country, then you must check for the following:

> a. The school that you intend to join must be approved by the FAA, CAA, JAA or any designated authority of the respective country to accept foreign students or Indian students.

b. The school should also assist you with the necessary documentation required for requesting a Student Visa for the duration of your training.
c. It should have arrangements or alternatives for your accommodation and meals of your choice.
d. At last but not the least, the school should provide your personal security, medical insurance, transportation to your school and back along with entertainment facilities. In fact, most of the foreign schools might provide these facilities to their students.
e. Never get in haste or make any hurry in deciding a school overseas. Investigate thoroughly about its authenticity and validity of the different certificates provided by the school in question and do also check the conversion procedures of the licenses earned from such schools to their Indian equivalent.

17. STUNNING ACCOMPLISHMENTS BY THE MAN IN AVIATION

Today, the aircraft we see or travel is much advanced and highly sophisticated. Earlier at the turn of 20th century when the World War I was in its full blow, the airplanes that took part in the war were not like today's masterpiece prototypes. They had two or even three wings called as "Biplanes" or "Tri-planes made up of woods and fabrics often with a blunt streamlining that offered lots of parasite drag. The pilots who used to fly these first generation aircrafts were also dare devils. There had been almost no assurance about the smooth running of the engines or normal working of the control surfaces. The pilots at those times often used to repair their airplanes by their own. If anything went wrong they had to make an emergency or crash landing and deal with the situation themselves. Some of these pilots had really broken the barrier of the real challenge lay in an engine-powered craft propelled not by strength but skill. The experiments of Orville Wright and Wilbur Wright, popularly known as "The Wright Brothers" in America and Alberto Santos-Dumont in France ironically opened the skies for the man to fly and explore a different world in the first self-propelled airplane. Since then the aviation progressed at mach speed and the man never looked back since then.

As the advancements and introduction of new technologies came through, aviation made a gigantic leap. The man in the form of Louis Bleriot had been the very first time able to cross the English Channel at 40 miles per hour through air. Gone were days when these dare devils had to fly the airplanes made from canvas, wood, bailing wire and crude navigation instruments which were almost to non-existent. The aviation technology was advancing with a revolutionary pace and made Chuck Yeager attempt to travel faster than the speed of sound and in 1947 he became the first human to travel with the Supersonic speed. Charles Lindbergh broke the Atlantic barrier and became the first human to fly from New York to Paris in less than 34 hours. Shortly thereafter in 1932, Amelia Earhart in her solo flight won the title of becoming the first woman to fly across the Atlantic. Each of these "Firsts" is a milestone in the history of aviation and it is no wonder that these aviators would always be recognized for opening the doors of the skies forever.

Experiments undertaken initially were often done by private individuals but very quickly it started attracting the public's attention. It took a few years for business organizations and the Governments to recognize the enormous potential of flight. Today when the aviation technology is reaching to its peak, the advantages of flight can be seen in almost every area like commerce, industry, transportation and national security. Earlier what looked extraordinary is now a piece of cake. Corporate executives can travel thousands of miles and get back home by the end of the day accomplishing their tasks. Packages and mails are swept across the country overnight and medicines and medical care of the patients can be reached to their places within a nick of a time.

With the advent of airplanes, the world has really become a small place to live and dream.

Printed in Great Britain
by Amazon